then grow cress seeds in the shells.

Growing your own food at home is fun and tasty.

So food doesn't have to travel a long way before you eat it.

I choose ...

Bamboo can be broken down naturally when it's finished with, which means it doesn't harm the environment.

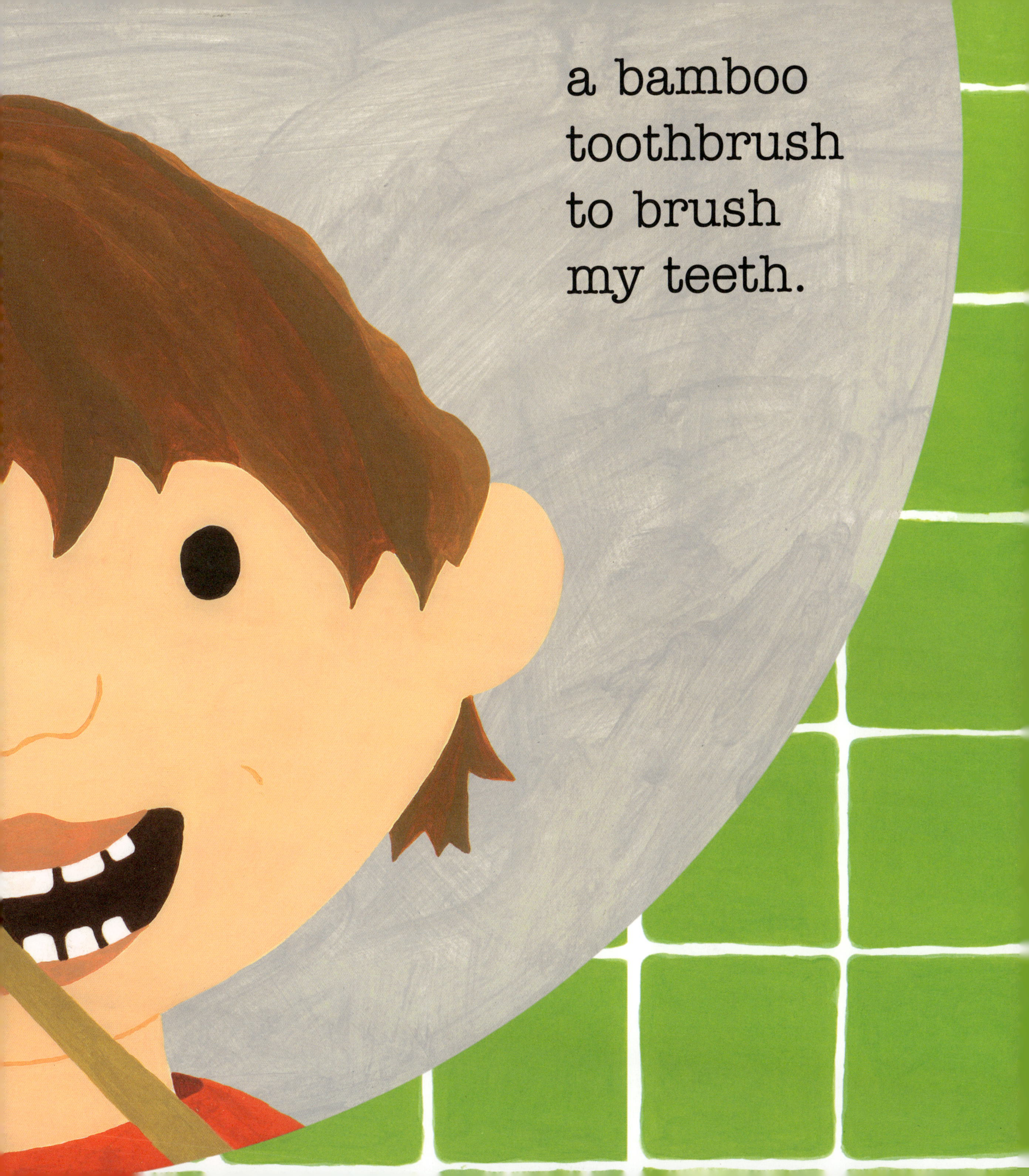

a bamboo
toothbrush
to brush
my teeth.

I enjoy …

making sock puppets
out of my old clothes.

It is fun to find new ways to use old things and reduce how much we throw away.

I pick out ...

vegetables at the market stall.

Buying loose fruit and vegetables from your local market means that you use less plastic packaging.

I always ...

I help ...

my mum to pack
leftovers for our lunch.

When we eat all the food that we cook, it helps reduce waste and save energy.

Reusable bottles can be used again and again without having to throw them away.

I’m happy …

taking the train when I go out.

Taking public transport like the bus or the train saves fuel and creates less pollution.

I remember ...

to take all
my things
home from
the beach.

Tidying away litter keeps the beach and sea clean and safe for animals.

I sort out ...

I can ...

make homes for local wildlife.